INGLÉS-ESPAÑOL BILINGÜE | ENGLISH-SPANISH BILINGUAL

1, 2, 3,

¿QUÉ VES?
WHAT DO YOU SEE?

Un libro de contar para niños pequeños
A Counting Book for Toddlers

Traducido por | Translated by Jocelyn M. Wood, MA, CCC-SLP

R

**ROCKRIDGE
PRESS**

Paperback ISBN: 979-8-88608-071-1
ebook ISBN: 979-8-88650-179-7

Manufactured in the United States of America

Series Designer: Darren Samuel
Interior and Cover Designer: Brieanna Felschow
Art Producer: Melissa Malinowsky
Editor: Sasha Henriques
Production Editor: Nora Milman
Production Manager: David Zapanta

Photography © iStock, cover and pp. 1, 7, 12, 16, 19, 20, 28-44; Shutterstock, cover and pp. 8, 11, 12, 15, 23, 24, 27

10 9 8 7 6 5 4 3 2 1 0

Este libro es de

This book belongs to

_____

Estimado lector/a:

El cerebro de su niño/a pequeño/a está creciendo tan rápido que no es extraño que la hora de la siesta sea un respiro bienvenido. A los 18 meses, los niños aprenden una palabra nueva cada dos horas que están despiertos. Su pequeño/a está constantemente adquiriendo un nuevo lenguaje y recibiendo nuevos estímulos.

Los estudios muestran que, aunque no tienen las palabras para expresarlo, los niños pequeños pueden comprender conceptos numéricos, identificar cantidades más grandes y más pequeñas e incluso hacer algunas restas básicas-¡antes de poder pedir más jugo!

Los niños pequeños están ávidos por aprender nuevos números y palabras. En este libro hemos juntado los conceptos básicos de contar con imágenes de objetos cotidianos que su hijo/a reconocerá y aprenderá a nombrar. Profundizará su experiencia de aprendizaje y despertará su imaginación, a la vez que disfrutará el tiempo que pasan juntos. ¡A contar se ha dicho!

Dear Reader,

Your toddler's brain is growing so fast that it's no wonder naptime is a welcome reprieve! By the time toddlers are 18 months old, they are learning one new word every two waking hours. Your little one is constantly absorbing new language and stimuli.

Studies show that although they don't have the words to express it, toddlers are able to understand numerical concepts, identify larger and smaller quantities, and even do some basic subtraction—all before they ask for more juice.

Toddlers are hungry to learn new numbers and words. Here, we've paired the counting basics with photos of everyday objects your child will recognize and learn to label. You'll deepen your child's learning experience and expand their imagination, all while cherishing time spent together. Happy counting!

uno
[OO-noh]

one

Uno gatito dormido

One sleepy kitty

2

dos
[DOHS]

two

Dos perritos felices
_____
Two happy puppies

3

tres
[TREHS]

three

Tres tiernos ositos de peluche

———

Three cuddly teddy bears

cuatro
[koo-AH-troh]

four

Cuatro camiones fuertes

Four tough trucks

5

cinco
[SEEN-koh]

five

Cinco vasos de plástico para bebé

———————

Five plastic sippy cups

6

seis
[SEH-ees]

six

Seis suéteres cómodos

———————

Six cozy sweaters

7

siete
[see-EH-teh]

seven

Siete patitos chillones

Seven squeaky ducks

ocho
[OH-choh]

eight

Ocho pelotas que rebotan

———

Eight bouncy balls

9

nueve   nine
[noo-EH-veh]

Nueve bloques coloridos
———————
Nine bright blocks

diez
[dee-EHS]

ten

Diez dedos sucios

Ten messy fingers

once
[OHN-seh]

eleven

Once rosquillas pegajosas

Eleven sticky donuts

doce
[DOH-seh]

twelve

Doce huevos pintos
———————
Twelve speckled eggs

trece
[TREH-seh]

thirteen

Trece galletas suaves
———
Thirteen chewy cookies

catorce   fourteen
[kah-TOHR-seh]

Catorce magdalenas pequeñitas
―――――
Fourteen mini muffins

quince
[KEEN-seh]

fifteen

Quince crayones
de colores

———

Fifteen colorful crayons

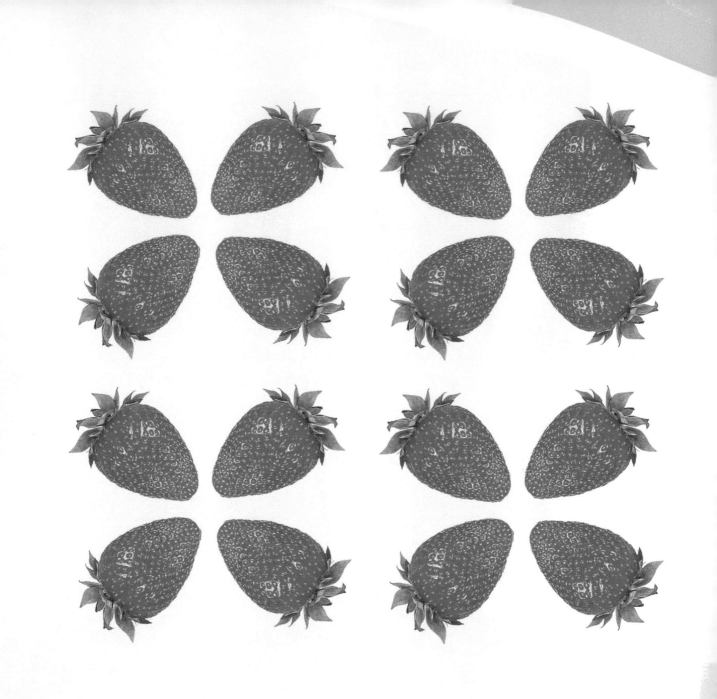

dieciséis
[dee-eh-see-SEH-ees]

sixteen

Dieciséis bayas jugosas
—————
Sixteen juicy berries

diecisiete   seventeen

[dee-eh-see-see-EH-teh]

Diecisiete piñas espinosas

Seventeen prickly pine cones

dieciocho
[dee-eh-see-OH-choh]

eighteen

Dieciocho hojas crujientes
———
Eighteen crunchy leaves

diecinueve   nineteen

[dee-eh-see-noo-EH-veh]

Diecinueve bellotas gordas
_____

Nineteen plump acorns

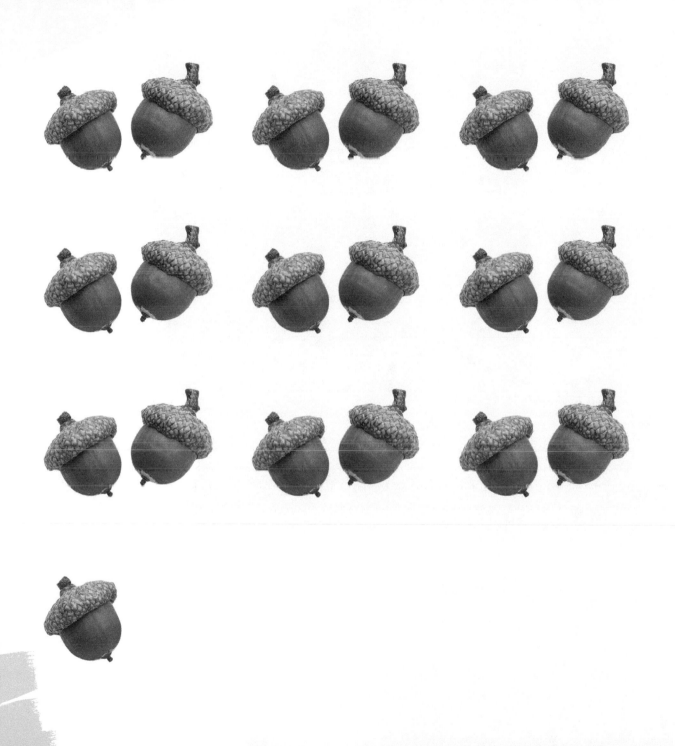

veinte
[VEH-een-teh]

twenty

Veinte flores delicadas

Twenty dainty flowers

Ayude a reforzar lo que su niño/a pequeño/a acaba de aprender haciendo juntos actividades divertidas para contar.

ACTIVIDAD DE PINTURA

Intente contar con una actividad divertida y sensorial. Ponga 20 gotitas pequeñas de pintura en una hoja de papel en blanco. Ponga cuidadosamente la página (mientras la pintura está húmeda) en una bolsa de plástico transparente con cierre hermético. Pídale a su hijo/a que aplaste cada gotita de pintura con el dedo mientras cuenta del 1 al 20.

HOJA DE NÚMEROS

Realice esta actividad para enseñarle a su niño/a a identificar los números. Reúna objetos pequeños, como pedacitos de cereal o pompones. En una hoja de papel, dibuje una cuadrícula con 20 casillas y numere cada una. Elija un número y pídale a su hijo/a que coloque esa cantidad de objetos en la casilla correspondiente. Cuenten a medida que avancen hasta llegar al número correcto. Cuando su hijo/a esté listo, hagan esta actividad sin las casillas.

Help reinforce what your toddler just learned with fun counting activities to do together.

SQUISH PAINT ACTIVITY

Try counting with a fun sensory activity. Place 20 small dollops of paint on a blank sheet of paper. Carefully seal the page (while the paint is still wet) in a clear, zip-top plastic bag. Have your child "squish" each paint dot with their finger while they count from 1 to 20.

NUMBER MAT

Use a number mat to teach your toddler number identification! Collect small objects, like cereal pieces or pom-poms. On a sheet of paper, draw a grid with 20 boxes and number each box. To play, pick a number and have your child place a small object into each box, counting up to the number as they go. When your child is ready, let them perform this activity without the boxes.

NÚMEROS / NUMBERS

1
uno
[OO-noh]
one

2
dos
[DOHS]
two

3
tres
[TREHS]
three

4
cuatro
[koo-AH-troh]
four

5
cinco
[SEEN-koh]
five

6
seis
[SEH-ees]
six

7
siete
[see-EH-teh]
seven

8
ocho
[OH-choh]
eight

9
nueve
[noo-EH-veh]
nine

10
diez
[dee-EHS]
ten

11 once *[OHN-seh]* eleven

12 doce *[DOH-seh]* twelve

13 trece *[TREH-seh]* thirteen

14 catorce *[kah-TOHR-seh]* fourteen

15 quince *[KEEN-seh]* fifteen

16 dieciséis *[dee-eh-see-SEH-ees]* sixteen

17 diecisiete *[dee-eh-see-see-EH-teh]* seventeen

18 dieciocho *[dee-eh-see-OH-choh]* eighteen

19 diecinueve *[dee-eh-see-noo-EH-veh]* nineteen

20 veinte *[VEH-een-teh]* twenty

ABECEDARIO / SPANISH ALPHABET

A [AH]	**B** [BEH]	**C** [SEH]	**CH** [CHEH]
D [DEH]	**E** [EH]	**F** [EH-feh]	**G** [HEH]
H [AH-cheh]	**I** [EE]	**J** [HOH-tah]	**K** [KAH]
L [EH-leh]	**LL** [EH-yeh]	**M** [EH-meh]	**N** [EH-neh]
Ñ [EH-nyeh]	**O** [OH]	**P** [PEH]	**Q** [KOO]
R [EH-reh]	**RR** [EH-rreh]	**S** [EH-seh]	**T** [TEH]
U [OO]	**V** [VEH]	**W** [DOH-bleh-veh]	**X** [EH-kees]
Y [YEH]	**Z** [SEH-tah]		

Printed in the USA
CPSIA information can be obtained
at www.ICGtesting.com
LVHW061345021223
765101LV00001B/8